MW00963491

Words
for
Encouragement

Poetry
by
Inge Claus

To order additional copies of this book, contact:
Xlibris Corporation
1-888-795-4274
www.Xlibris.com
Orders@Xlibris.com
123615

To my Children
Berni and Elke,
my Grandsons
Kulan and Jethro
and Great-grandson Kolby

Dear Reader:

This is my third book with 100 inspirational poems. I started writing poems at the age of 80 years and finished my first little poem book in spring 2004. A second book followed in the summer 2005. It took me a little longer to finish my third book due to the preparation for moving to another house and a tough time because of health problems. But this didn't stop me to continue to express my feelings in poetry. It is a great help when going through difficult times, but too, I like to express my gratitude when experience joy in living.

As before, in my poems I like to be honest with my feelings. The inspirations come from my faith in Almighty God and are an expression of gratitude for His guiding light along the journey of my life.

May you here and there find a poem that speaks to your heart and might give you hope and encouragement.

Inge Claus, 2012

Acknowledgement:

My faithful friend Jean Gowland from my writing class, again, for the third time, combed through my poems carefully to improve grammar and spelling. Despite her 91 years of age, her mind is sharp and her English excellent. My gratitude and thanks go to this friend for spending for me valuable hours. In addition, I like to express my thankfulness to Hanne Neumeister, I know from former employment, who too took time to look over my poems. I am surely in debt to friends like these.

As before, my son Berni is always readily available with his help when I have computer questions. What would I do without him?

And above all, and not to forget, my thanks, gratitude and love go to my Creator who helped me with my writing by giving me inspiration and as well joy in writing.

Poetry is the voice of the soul whispering, celebrating, singing even.

Carolyn Forche'

Contents

1. The Greatest Treasure of all

Treasures are not easy to find;
we must search for them with our heart and mind.
But what is the treasure that surpasses all,
on which we day and night can call?

It is God's presence in our heart
that we never want from us to depart,
that leads us out of darkness into His light
and guides us by His truth so bright.

When following His will with eagerness,
we will know joy because our Maker does us bless.
In His love and care we shall feel secure
when of His presence we are sure.

Indeed, to be close to our Saviour
let us not in vain labour.
His presence we never can value highly enough,
since by it we dwell securely in His love.

2. When Heaven touches the Soul

Heaven seems to be so far away
and yet it can be close to us when to the Lord we pray,
or it might be that heavenly music touches our soul
and for a little while we feel that we are whole.

Music, indeed, to Heaven may us uplift;
it surely is one of God's precious gifts.
It might bring tears to our eyes,
and we know the Saviours love for us are no lies.

Forgotten are struggles and pain for awhile
and far away seems any trial.
We are transported over clouds far above
and our hearts are filled with gratitude and love.

But to come back to earth we are bound,
yet, we will savour the moment when heaven we found.
It will help us not to fear our life's end,
since glorious time awaits us
when our life in heaven we spend.

3. The Foolishness Of God

Many men think they are wise and smart
when they do not listen to their heart.
They like to reach heaven by their own effort
and think for this they do not need the Lord.

Full of pride they look down on the weak
who know without the help of God the world looks bleak,
who humbly ask Him their ways to guide
and in darkness to give them light.

But the self-confident think they find their way alone
and reject the King on the heavenly throne.
God's way of salvation is foolishness to them
and with this they do themselves condemn.

They think they are intelligent and wise
and believe many of Satan's deceitful lies,
rejecting the love the Lord showed us on the cross
giving His life for our sins at such a great loss.

God might seem foolish when He chooses
a person unknown and weak,
who is willing to serve Him in word and deed.
But, all the wisdom of men the wise God will destroy
and the intelligence of the intelligent annoy.

God's foolishness is wiser than all the wisdom of mankind
and wise is the man who searches the Saviour's wisdom to find,
who relies on Him in all his ways,
since he knows the knowledge of man always betrays.

4. Wisdom

Wisdom is more precious than silver or gold,
which a wise man as his greatest treasure does hold.
To find it we have to ask the Lord
to reveal it to us in His Word.

God's wisdom and truth in the Bible we find;
we not only discover that our Saviour is kind,
that His advice is sound and of great wealth,
and when obeying brings peace and health.

The Proverbs in God's Word we should heed;
to a contented life they will lead.
Our searching the Scriptures will never be in vain
and day by day more wisdom we might gain.

How to pity an unbelieving man
who thinks, finding wisdom by himself he can,
not realising that he is surrounded by the dark
and his feet are stumbling when he does walk.

Let us in gratitude to our Maker turn
and with passion for His wisdom yearn.
Let us obey His perfect will,
so we find peace and can be still.

5. Your greatest Friend

Oh child of God, why are you so dismayed
don't you know that Jesus His life
on the cross for you laid?
It is the greatest sacrifice to give
and this He did it that you might live.

He promised never you to forsake
and always by His hand He will you take.
He promised to leave you never,
in sickness and health He will be with you forever.

Gold has to be refined by the Master's hand
so be not discouraged when
the heat you are unable to stand.
You will come forth as the purest of gold
when the Lord has finished you to mould.

Be encouraged that our Redeemer cares so much for you,
His love is unconditional and true.
Be assured God will bring good out of your trial,
so you can take courage and rest awhile.

6. Resurrection

In every flower we can see resurrection in spring,
which hope of a new beginning does bring.
Why do so many people believe life has an end
and in hopelessness their days are spend.

God's Word tell us over and over again
that life has a purpose and we don't live in vain.
It tells us of many witnesses who
Christ's Resurrection have seen,
who ate with Him, touched Him
and in His presence have been.

Since God's Word is never false and always true,
because Jesus was raised to life again,
so will His followers be, too.
Let's sink in our hearts this news that is so great
and believe our Redeemer died for us on the Cross,
before it is too late.

7. God Cares!

When the sky seems to be dark,
God cares!
When you don't hear the song of the lark,
God cares!

When you think you are all alone,
God cares!
When hurting in every bone,
God cares!

When everything goes well,
God cares!
When of His greatness you like others to tell,
God cares!

When on your way are problems and trials,
God cares!
When your faith is dim and long seem the miles,
God cares!

The Lord cares in all situations,
He is near you in all locations.
He watches over you night and day,
His care is never ending along your journey's way.

8. 'Father' – What a precious Name

To have a Father in the heaven's above
speaks of trust, security and love.
We know that His children He will guide
with His wisdom and His might.

We can feel content and secure
and of His loving hand can be sure.
We are protected by His care
and always He is loving and fair.

We often don't see that He wants for our life the best
and even doubt Him when He does us bless.
His discipline we like to shun,
which He uses in order that more like Jesus we become.

Precious Heavenly Father let us adore you every hour,
let us look up to your love and power.
Help us to be obedient to your will,
and rest in your care and to be still.

9. Let's stand in Awe before our Creator

In awe we should stand before God's majesty and power;
God rules with justice and loves us each single hour.
He is our rock, who doesn't change and is everlasting,
on Him all our burdens we can be casting.

With all our hearts let us praise our King;
rejoice in His love and to Him let us sing.
He wants us to follow Him and to obey,
so that our life is fruitful and we do not stray.

Praising Almighty God does lift us up,
it certainly fills to the brim our cup.
With wonder we embrace His unconditional love,
which He so abundantly sheds from the heaven's above.

Our heart will flow over with thankfulness,
when we are aware how much God does us bless,
when we realise that He provides for all our needs,
so let us praise Him in words and with deeds.

10. God's Grace

Grace is a free gift that cannot be earned,
humbly to receive it, it has to be learned.
It cannot be worked for nor come on request,
we receive it from God, with whose love we've been
blessed.

Before Jesus' cross we all stand as sinners,
for here are no losers and nor are there winners.
The respectful and murderers are all in need
to receive our Creator's grace that from sin us freed.

So let us in God's forgiveness rejoice
and start in the book of life a clean page of our choice.
Let us rejoice that His beloved children we'll be,
remembering, it is by God's grace and completely free.

11. The Light that guides us

Jesus is the world's guiding light,
which shines so brightly during the night.
It guides our too unsteady feet
and let's see any good and evil deed.

And yet, many in the darkness like to live
refusing the guidance that Christ does give;
they prefer to go their own confusing way
and walking in darkness every day.

But when Jesus we do obey
from the right path we will not stray.
His light will guide us in every trial
so we are able to walk unafraid many a mile.

12. Give Praises to the Lord

The Lord is to be praised above everything,
because He is our Creator, Redeemer and King.
He rules with a firm and loving hand,
so that in awe before Him all creation should stand.

His love is unconditional and never ending;
with compassion His help He always is lending.
Let us praise Him for abundantly filling our need
and for directing us in both word and in deed.

He never gets tired of guiding our way;
He wants us to cling to Him and not to go astray.
Let us praise and worship Him for healing our soul
and changing us so that we become whole.

13. Remember God's Faithfulness

When clouds darken our day,
when slow and difficult seems the way,
God's mercy then we should recall,
His guidance and His love for all.

When tears stream down our face,
when hopeless seems to be our case,
Then let's sing a song of praise to the Most High,
so that this will end our cry.

New hope then will flow through our heart
and again joy finally has a new start.
With new energy we can do every task
and for the Lord's presence is all we ask.

We feel safe when He is taking our hand
and when every hour with Him we spend.
Our hearts then are filled with gratefulness
and we realise that God always wants us to bless.

14. Remember God's Protection

When life is difficult and tough,
when the road is steep and rough,
when you are near to giving up,
then remember that the Lord has always filled your cup.

Remember that He has protected you from harm,
and that never too short was found His strong arm,
that He guided you by night and day,
that from the narrow path you'd not stray.

These thoughts should give you strength when facing
trials,
when the road seems long having too many miles.
So that now with courage you climb your hill
until reaching the summit, when you can rest and be still.

15. Decisions

Decisions are not always easy to make,
sometimes there are risks we might have to take.
Take advice from some friend who has earned your trust,
though praying about it is always a must.

To make a decision is often a struggle,
it might give us all kinds of trouble,
it might involve those to us dear
who wrong decisions by us fear.

In our lives sometimes God has closed up a door,
because he has something much better for us in store.
Yet, if His perfect Word we obey,
complete peace of mind will then with us stay.

16. When the Battle is won

We're involved in battles during all of our life
because there is not only harmony, but much too often
strife.
We get weary when war never comes to an end
and precious time with fighting we have to spend.

For peaceful moments we must pray and hope,
to enjoy the beauty around us in order to cope.
Yet, the battle for us is so often discouraging;
our strength is in looking to Jesus our King.

Wars do take much of our strength
since most of the time they go on for quite a length.
But, the Lord stays close by His children's fight
and sustaining them ever with His love and His might.

When the battle is over and finally won,
we give praise to God for what He has done.
Without shouting in joy, we have the calm assurance,
that God fought for us through His gift of endurance.

17. Lost in a Jungle

Have you ever felt that in a jungle you are lost
and looked for some light at any cost.
Have you ever felt lost in a big city not finding your way
and the many streets from the right turn let you stray.

Have you ever felt like losing your mother's hand
or being alone without any friend?
Then you know how many people do feel,
having no hope someone would help them heal.

In their lost state they struggle day and night
and are not able to see any light.
They think life's success depend only on them alone
and they don't cry out to the heavenly throne.

If only one would tell them about our Saviour
who is so willing to help in all our labour.
He waits for us even when in faith we lack
and takes us in His fold in order to protect.

Our jungle with His light He penetrates,
since the darkness of our sins He greatly hates.
He will lead us in all our ways
and takes our fear not from Him to stray.

18. Writer's Block

Nothing of value enters my mind,
no thoughts of wisdom or thoughts that are kind.
Impatient I hold the pen in my hand;
does not anyone some help me lend?

I stare into space frustrated
and hope that ideas will be created,
but there is a block in my head,
it is as if my mind is dead.

Maybe a refreshing sleep chases the block away,
and so hopefully on my bed I lay.
Yet, the next day is no different
although many hours slumbering I spent.

I realise, patient I have to be,
to my problem that might be the key.
Then suddenly on a clear sunny day
the writer's block disappears and goes away.

With new energy I go on to write
and fill page after page that has been blank and white.
Joy fills my heart that my thoughts freely flow
and in gratitude my head I bow low.

19. Unkind Words

Unkind words are so easily used,
they hurt and many a person with these is abused.
Words can cut deep in someone's heart
like an arrow that is sharp.

Often some people like to hurt those
that to them are very close.
Why do they reject the love that to them is extended?
Hurtful words need time to be mended.

Even if not holding a grudge and being forgiving,
wounds have to heal before enjoying living.
Unkind words are often not realised
by those who do them use,
but kindness is better to choose.

20. The Struggle to Rest

Our days are crowded with activities,
not only with work that brings pay and fees.
We tend to think the world will stand still
when we are not busy and exercise our will.

We don't take time to have a needed rest
and think being busy is for us the best.
Even when the Lord through afflictions
likes to slow us down,
we murmur and like to wear a frown.

Illness often forces us to take a needed break
and we struggle and think with
our work we will be late.
But our wise Creator knows what for us is the best
and we are forced through illness to take a rest.

We might learn to be still
and appreciate God's perfect will.
We might learn to have balance of work and rest each day,
otherwise with fatigue and sickness we have to pay.

So let us try to take a pause in our daily labour
and enjoy a relaxing hour with a neighbour.
Let us sit still and listen to a little bird's song;
taking a rest once in a while will never prove wrong.

21. Sadness

The sun is shining and yet I am sad.
What is it that I feel so bad?
Why do I shed some tears,
although I don't have any fears?

Why am I so full of sorrow,
will it last until tomorrow?
Those who are happy, they are from me far,
I am not able to see any star.

But when I think that Jesus by His love
wants me to bless,
it fills my heart with thankfulness.
With His help those who hurt me
I will be able to forgive,
because for my Saviour my passion is to live.

22. When Illness strikes

Health is a precious thing
although it not always does happiness bring.
We take it for granted without any thought,
some even think with money it can be bought.

But continuous sunshine let us stand still
and is never in God's divine will.
As a perfect gardener He knows
that we need rain for our growth.

He knows how much He has to prune,
and we think it is for our doom.
But more fruit we will produce in the end
though illness for the child of God not in vain is spend.

23. Downcast

Why are you downcast oh my soul,
is it because you are far from being whole,
is it because you failed again
and your efforts seemed to be all in vain?

Or does the rain weight heavy on your heart
and you don't hear the singing of a lark?
There seemed to be none who might understand,
who to you a listening ear could lend.

Oh no, there is one, who is always there for you,
who knows how you feel and what you do,
who cares for you day in and out
in quiet comforting words without a doubt.

Jesus is the one who does understand;
He is the one who His ear to you does lend.
He understands when we fail and are cast down,
when we are not rejoicing and are wearing a frown.

To know that He cares and does us love
will let us see our blessings from above.
It will chase the dark clouds away
and let us rejoice at the end of the day.

24. Self-Indulgence

Why am I so utterly weak
and overcoming my indulgence looks so bleak?
I feel ashamed to tell any other
what it is that really does me bother.

Variety I love, I like to say,
but with this the real reason I do betray;
to buy sweaters galore I am not able to resist,
and to count them would make a very long list.

Am I vain that I hoard them day after day,
more rewarding would be to give them away.
Who can save me from this indulgence of mine,
will I never be able temptation to decline?

And so I struggle with this weakness
already for many a year;
I love my sweaters which are to me dear.
I wonder if it is grave a sin
and if my indulgence encourages the next of kin?

I realise that my own will is not very strong
and then I am uncertain if I am wrong.
Surely, I have to admit that I am not perfect at all
and that my human weaknesses let's sometimes me fall.

25. Weakness

Like eagles we like to fly
up toward the heaven's sky.
We don't like to take any rest
and think without pause we are at our best.

We wish we would never be tired or weak
when the sun seems hidden and the day looks bleak,
when all we must do seems an effort great
and we're left to complain that our tasks finish late.

But our great Physician knows what for us is best
and knows that some times we need a rest.
Being weak and tired might then lead us think
that to rely on the Lord, new strength let's us bring.

Our days are not always the same,
some days we are tired and
on others more energy we gain.
Yet if with both sunshine and rain
God wants us to bless,
let us accept each day with thankfulness.

26. Disappointments

Disappointment will come everyone's way,
even when believing that God's Will we do obey.
God's prophets had opposition galore
and often thought they could not take this anymore.

Yet despite their distress, in the Lord they kept trust;
for them to follow His truth was a must.
All too often those whom we love our Saviour they reject
and searching in His Word they decide to neglect.

Our hearts will always go out for them,
and it is not for us our loved ones to condemn.
We pray that one day they will see God's might
that penetrates their souls with His light.

We like them to see that only through
Jesus Christ comes salvation,
that through His death on the cross
there is for us no condemnation.
But to take His outstretched hand is anyone's choice
and over each repented sinner the Heaven's rejoice.

27. In the Desert

For constant sunshine we do yearn,
but then any fruit we wouldn't earn.
So often of this truth we are not aware
and we think that walking in a desert is not fair.

There in circles we seem to go
and our hope is very low
to find ever alone our way
until we realise from God's guidance we did stray.

Then in our distress to an unknown God we cry
to give us purpose for life or we die,
to lead us out of the wilderness
and ask with rich pastures us to bless.

For this God patiently has waited;
our rejection of Him He had hated;
He likes to see that for everything on Him we depend
and do willingly for our sins repent.

Then He will guide our walk
and we are led out of the dark,
so that joy and thankfulness fills our heart
and life for us does have a new start.

28. Feeling Low

I can't understand why I am downcast today;
the people around me are kind and didn't me betray.
But I feel alone and for myself sorry,
although I have no need to worry.

I want only my own company,
to think and wonder how unfriendly I can be.
It is not my intention to hurt those nearby,
but to understand my feelings results in a big 'Why'.

There is only one who truly does me understand,
who always is there for me with His outstretched hand.
My mood lifts up when thinking of Jesus' love for me,
who gave His life for my sins on a dreadful tree.

Thankfulness slowly fills my heart
and feelings of gratitude start;
the world now looks brighter again,
indeed, God's love is never in vain.

29. Why do I cry today?

Why is so low my mood;
for my sadness, what might be the root?
I like to shed many tears,
despite I don't have any fears.

I think, I don't like being of energy so low,
everything is an effort and I am very slow.
The Bible says that God loves the weak,
but why then does the day look so bleak?

I believe that my Creator does care for me;
I know that He gave His life for my sins on a tree.
So, I certainly have no reason to be sad,
because God loves me , I should rejoice and be glad.

Understanding the human heart is no easy task,
our Maker is the only one who understands
and Him we should ask.
He will tell us our feelings we should never trust,
and that to love and obey Him for us is a must.

30. Tired of Pain

Pain does discourage and is tiring
and we seem to cease the beauty around us admiring.
We struggle each single day
and hope that the pain does go away.

We wonder if there is any purpose in our pain,
if any more wisdom from it we might gain?
If of this we could be sure,
then maybe more patiently we would endure.

To the outside world we like to be seen as strong
and we think our discouragement is wrong;
we like to see the end of the tunnel dark
and enjoy again the sunshine and the song of a lark.

In all our discomfort let us never forget
of God's past mercy and grace He did on us shed.
Let us never forget His promises so great
and that His healing will never be too late.

31. Fatigue

Why am I so fatigued,
and all the time feel tired and weak?
Everything requires an effort and is a chore,
those around me must think I'm a bore.

Even cleaning my teeth is a difficult task I find,
and clouded seems to be my mind.
Should I be patient for a longer while?
How long will it take until the end comes of my trial?

When forcing myself to do some task,
wondering why I feel a little better, I ask.
Are my 84 years the reason I'm weak,
when three days ago the day seemed less bleak.

I pray that the Lord will help me with my affliction to cope
and let me live with unfailing hope,
to let me be assured that He turns out everything for the best
and that in the end He will me bless.

32. Affliction

How long will my trials last?
I know Lord that I shouldn't ask.
I have read about people, who have courage when ill,
who are accepting and have peace and are still.

But I am no hero of this special kind
and hope my trials don't make me unkind.
If I could only feel that you're on my side,
then the days would be easier for me to abide.

Why are you so far away?
I long for you when I do pray.
My hope lies in your promises and love,
let blessings rain on me from the heaven's above.

33. When Clouds hide the Sun

Why today clouds affect my mood
and tasteless seems to be all food?
I am slow as a snail;
will my downcast mood prevail?

Nothing seems to lift me up
and I feel sorry for my cup.
I don't like doing anything,
Just wanting to sit still and think.

The Lord seems to be so far away
and yet I know He is with me every day.
I just don't realise His presence,
does He want to teach me a lesson?

Does He want to teach me that not all days
are sunny and gay,
and that sometimes steeper is the way?
that He gives me strength for today and tomorrow
so that joy again will replace my sorrow.

34. When the Road is steep

Steep sometimes is the path before our feet;
as moving forward we can't leap.
Discouraged, to give up we might like,
since endless seems to be the hike.

But with climbing we have to go on,
although we don't see in it any fun.
We just cannot stand still,
because for us we know that going
forward is God's will.

A rest we can allow ourselves to take
and hope that we are not much too late.
We notice that other hikers are weary too,
for they struggle like we sometimes do.

From experience we know the road is not always steep
and that for us beautiful views us on the narrow way keep.
We know that hope again will flow into our brain
and that all the climbing hasn't been in vain.

35. In the Valley

When in the valley, we feel alone,
far away seems to be God's throne.
We weep and heavy is our heart
and with hopeful steps long to re-start.

God's mercy then we should remember,
His guidance and His love so tender.
We trust Him to lead us through the valley so dark,
so once again we hear the song of the lark.

Our hearts then are joyful again
and forgotten is all the pain.
But the experience made us grow
and in thankfulness to the Lord our
heads we bow low.

36. Waiting for a Cancer Test Result

July 11, 2007

Will the news be good or bad?
I wish the results I already had.
Worrying about it would be a waste of time,
today I feel well and tomorrow I might also be fine.

I know that my Saviour will never leave or forsake me;
He showed His love as He was crucified on a tree.
And yet my mind is not quite still,
wondering what might be God's will.

That all goes well for those who do Jesus love
is a promise from above.
Oh, that I would trust Him without doubting at all,
that despite my uncertainty I would still stand tall.

Tomorrow I will know my fate,
for then no longer need I wait.
God will give me strength to accept the result of the test;
from life experience I know for me it will be the best.

37. Ice Cubes

Feelings after major surgery

Who would trade a diamond for a little cube of ice,
would people do this just to be nice,
would they not be considered out of their mind?
But I can tell you that such people you might find.

When going off to the hospital for major surgery
in an anxious mood;
and when one day before, you are allowed to have only
liquid food,
when after surgery you can only on a few ice cubes sip
to moisten, oh, your very dry lip.

Then how wonderfully cool to you this does taste,
wearing a diamond instead seems such a waste.
It wouldn't keep you from craving something wet,
then at this moment you would trade a diamond
for a little ice cube instead.

38. When Darkness engulfs you

Written in hospital after Urostomy Surgery
on July 30, 2007

Where is the light, where is a star?
Night engulfs the universe near and far.
How can I find my way when utterly lost,
what is the price, what is the cost?

God hides far behind the clouds
and seems not to care to heal my wounds.
He seems to be leaving me all alone
and doesn't step down from His heavenly throne.

The evil one laughs in my face,
and desperately I long for God's grace.
As dawn approaches, the darkness lifts
and glimmers of hope come to me as gifts.

Darkness has to give way to light
and slowly hope replaces my plight.
A new morning is starting upon its way
and with a thankful heart I pray.

39. A long Night

I long for a refreshing sleep,
but when older your slumber is seldom deep.
So, restless I lay in my bed
and wish some more hours of sleep I had.

Reading might pass the time,
and I wonder if tomorrow I shall feel fine.
Eagerly I wait for dawn to end the night
and to enjoy once again the day's wonderful light.

I might get tired sometime in the day
and hope that catching up on sleep I may.
Will the next night be so long once again,
and will my prayers have been all in vain?

But complaining surely would not be wise,
much better to let our courage rise.
Let us every waking hour enjoy
and hope that our Lord does us employ.

40. Doubting God

When around us dark is the night,
when we are unable to discover any light,
when suffering seems too much to bear
and we are closest to despair.

Then doubt about God's love might cross our mind
and we wonder why to us the Lord seems so unkind.
We just cannot stand anymore the pain
and wonder if our suffering is all in vain.

The night doesn't want to end
and by doubting God, life seems in hell to spend.
Shall we hold fast what the Bible does us tell,
that God won't forsake us and to an end
comes this present hell?

41. Discouragement

Why today is discouraged my soul;
I seem to be so far from being whole.
Just yesterday, I accomplished many a task,
why not today, I like to ask.

Why does my mood go up and down,
sometimes I smile and other times wear a frown.
some days, myself I can't understand
and wished I would always be content.

Only by trusting my Saviour have I hope
and are able with discouraging thoughts to cope.
Jesus is both my rock and my strength
and for this my heart should be penitent.

42. Feeling Sorry for myself

I felt like crying this morning as I woke up;
why did I think quite empty is my cup,
why didn't I greet the day on a thankful note,
why did I feel I have to travel a very steep road?

Was my mood affected by the steady snow and rain?
Or did I feel sorry for myself because of some pain?
Did linger still in my mind
some unkind word from my spouse,
could all this be the cause?

A new day is a gift from our Saviour,
for whom in gladness I should labour.
He wants me to see His love each day,
so that my mood will change
when with gratitude to Him I pray.

Often our feelings we don't understand;
it is good when we talk about it to a friend.
But never let's forget that Jesus always gives a listening ear,
because each soul He loves and to Him is dear.

43. Using our Gifts

Each one of us is given talents and skills from above
which we should develop with patience and love.
But when neglecting our gifts,
our purpose in life we will miss.

Too often duties all our hours seem to take
and we are unable for our skills time to make.
Then frustrations might fill our day
and through loss of energy we might have to pay.

To do the things we love, can it be called selfishness,
even when sure, God in our work does greatly us bless.
Shall we ever be able our priorities to see,
which from guilty feelings would set us free?

Only by talking with the Lord we will know
the way He desires us to go.
Yet, it is not always easy to know God's will,
so that our hearts are content and we learn to be still.

44. Feeling Safe

People are looking for security;
they would buy it even when it cost a great fee.
They want to feel safe in their employment
and think that this is needed for life's enjoyment.

Children should have the security of their parent's love,
and most of us don't realise that we can feel safe
in our Heavenly Father from above.
He likes to hide us under His wings
which, peace of mind to us brings.

We cannot earn this by striving diligently,
only by taking refuge in our Maker willingly,
by relying on Him night and day
and being eager to Him to pray.

Without Him we never will be secure,
having difficulty all the world's changes to endure.
But God who never changes is our rock,
and we will be safe in Him even if someone does us mock.

45. The Blessings of Old Age

Are there blessings in old age?
Can we recall joyful moments that might fill a page;
are there not health problems that weigh us down,
that make us discouraged and wear a frown?

But when we are honest we will recall
that in our youth we had many a fall.
We were not always happy and in a joyful mood,
we often were starving for spiritual food.

We took for granted when God did us bless
and were not always thankful, I guess.
But in old age we might have learned
to rejoice in a small thing
that gratitude to our heart did bring.

We might be thankful for a good sleep at night
or when the rain stops and the sun shines bright,
when we have a day without pain
or a new friendship did gain.

We might rejoice for the gift of each new day
in which the Lord guides us in His way.
There is still purpose in the life of a person who is old
as we in the Word of our Creator are told.

So, never let us despair when failing is our health,
a long life can have indeed great wealth.
We might have learned more and more in God to rejoice
and know that to love the Lord is our choice.

46. Love your Neighbour as Yourself

If we want to care for our neighbour
we have to be willing to embrace the love of our Saviour.
Only when we really feel His acceptance in our heart,
then loving ourselves and others will have had a start.

That doesn't mean to be with ourselves absorbed,
which is always selfish and morbid.
A healthy self-love calls for respect
and the knowledge that the Lord values us is a fact.

In His great love on the cross His blood He shed
so that through this salvation we might get.
Who are we then, not ourselves to love and to accept,
we are free and paid is our debt.

Only when we accept ourselves with warts and all
are we able with love on our neighbour to call.
Not only this, we can be sure that God never will us
forsake,
because out of His love He did us create.

47. To be a Servant

We shy away from being a servant to one another;
rather do our own thing and have no-one us to bother.
Serving means to lay our selfishness aside
as well our giving up time and pride.

Recently, I watched many servants at a hospital stay,
as I had cancer surgery and to the Lord I did pray.
He opened my eyes to see in the nurses their serving love
and I knew their work was blessed from the heavens
above.

One nurse was as beautiful as the other,
and in their simple work clothes
with fashion they did not bother.
They did their duty with encouragement and a smile
and made me comfortable as I rested for awhile.

That made me realise that I am often a poor servant
when for others I have to do a simple errand.
I love to do things that can be seen,
and for ordinary daily tasks I am not so keen.

I hope God helps me to listen to His teaching
so that more to closeness with Him I am reaching.
What wonderful lessons He likes to give us again and
again,
expecting that His training of us is not all in vain.

48. Little Joys

There are many small things in life to enjoy;
we just have to watch a little girl or boy.
But when we get older we demand more and more
and we neglect little things and find them a bore.

Nevertheless, when white hair crowns our head
and through health problems a different life must be led,
we might start enjoying things which before we ignored
and now learn for instance that a quiet hour can be adored.

We might rejoice that we still can walk,
be able to hear and to talk.
We might be thankful still to be able
to perform some daily chores,
to start something new or open new doors.

We might view every day as a challenge to meet,
and rejoice that with purpose we might be complete.
We might look back on a long life with thankfulness
and realise that through all our struggles God did us bless.

49. When Kindness seems to be cruel

Cruel can be sickness and pain,
and dumbness and deafness or being lame.
We think life's best we will experience never,
yet, to give up would not be very clever.

We must realise that in a fallen world we live
where selfishness is the norm and people aren't eager to
give.
God wants us to grow to become like His Son
and that is painful and in a hurry can't be done.

Our sin is like a cancer that can us destroy;
it causes us pain that does us annoy.
But like a kind surgeon, God wants the cancer in us cut
out
and He might seem to be cruel when in our pain we cry
about.

Yet our Maker never causes us pain
that doesn't bring healing to His children
and would be in vain.
So let us endure His skilled kind hand
and embrace His love that has no end.

50. Beauty

Beauty we can see every day,
even when steep is our way.
But it depends if our eyes are open and clear
and we are aware of the beauty that to us is near.

We don't have to go far away,
beauty is all around us to stay.
A little bird might enjoy us with a song,
even when this delight doesn't last very long.

And then who wouldn't admire a rose
when not resting our eyes on the thorns too close.
A colourful rainbow can our eyes excite,
although rain had produced this delight.

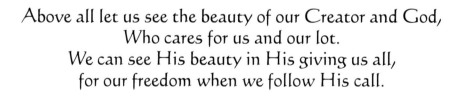

There is beauty in encouraging words,
that helps us to cope of one of our hurts.
There is beauty in a hug and a smile,
even if it last only a little while.

Above all let us see the beauty of our Creator and God,
Who cares for us and our lot.
We can see His beauty in His giving us all,
for our freedom when we follow His call.

51. A glorious Day

On the seventh day of creation God took a rest
commanding us to do the same, because it is for us the
best.
Yet people are shopping on this lovely day
and then with exhaustion they have to pay.

Taking a rest on a Sunday is a break from our daily chore,
and then for the week we shall gain strength once a bit
more.
So let us enjoy rest at the end of the week,
it surely is more then an ordinary treat.

This glorious day we should embrace
to refresh our mind and body by God's grace.
We could enjoy reading an uplifting book
or admiring a flower with a closer look.

Listening to music may speak to our heart;
we don't have always to study in order to be smart.
Let us worship our Heavenly Father on this special day,
so that peace, joy and contentment will with us stay.

52. My favourite Hour

Early in the morning I like to rise,
wondering if God for me has any surprise.
This early hour is wonderfully quiet
when not completely has passed the night.

In the summer I see the dawn changing to light
and the sun on some days shining so bright.
My heart might be filled with hope and thankfulness
that the Lord with the gift of a new day did me bless.

After breakfast I spend an hour in the presence of my Saviour
asking Him to give me strength for
the day's duty and labour.
In His written Word I love myself to immerse
to take in the wisdom of His precious verse.

There are days when a new truth I discover
and see more clearly that Jesus is mankind's lover.
But on other days I might struggle with the learning
as for more insight I am desperately yearning.

My prayers might be filled with adoration and awe,
because I see the beauty of God's Law.
But not every day my heart is soft and filled with
gratefulness
and then I don't realise that God me always wants to bless.

Yet, the morning hour spent with my Creator
strengthens me during the hours later.
I never would like to miss this time any day,
hoping to understand more what the Lord to me has to say.

53. When Joy visits us

We don't have to lie on an exotic beach
or, in a lottery, win one million dollars reach,
we don't need in our marriage always support,
but surely we have to know the love of the Lord.

If we experience His love so deep,
for joy we like to weep.
With thankfulness we lift up our eyes
and praise the Almighty in the skies.

Even when on our way we have trials
and have to walk a number of miles,
when we know our Creator's faithfulness,
we will trust Him that He wants us to bless.

Joy might surprise us when doing our daily work
and even when life might badly us hurt,
on circumstances it doesn't depend,
but only what time in God's presence we spend.

54. The Beauty of Heaven

We cannot picture in our mind
what beauty in Heaven we shall find.
We think of paradise as the most wonderful place,
where we can only enter through our Redeemer's grace.

Love will rule there forever
and it doesn't matter if we are not clever.
Although the personalities of God's children
different you can call,
still, there is harmony amongst them all.

No evil in God's presence we have to fear
and always our conscience will be clear.
We will be able with a lion to play
and this animal won't harm us in any way.

Above all, to Jesus we can talk
and enjoy with Him to walk.
We will love to work and worship the King of kings,
who great joy to us forever brings.

55. When the Sun breaks through

The birds awaken with their song
after a dark night so long.
Could it be that the sun warms the earth again
and the long night of waiting was not all in vain?

New energy is flowing through my veins
and all forgotten are my difficult pains.
New life awakens my heart
and new dreams are making a start.

I like to sing with the birds
and hope to have learned from my hurts.
What wanted my Creator me to teach
as He bent down my hand to reach?

A tough lesson He surely gave,
and I thought I was near my grave.
But now new hope does me surround,
and the assurance of His love I found.

56. The Beauty of a Rest

When the pace is fast and along we hurry,
then we are anything but merry.
We don't seem to have time for some rest
and then I doubt, we are doing our best.

Why is it that we think the days are too short?
If that was the case, more hours
would have provided the Lord.
He only asks for work done according to our strength
and the days are sufficient for it by their length.

He doesn't want us to hurry without any pause,
that might for an illness be the cause.
He likes us to see the beauty of reflection and rest,
and surely, I think, we are then able to do our best.

57. A day with Energy

When young you take energy for granted;
it's not top on the list of the desperately wanted.
The picture changes when you are old and grey is your hair
and you think your lack of energy isn't fair.

Tiredness might plague you many a day
and for more strength to the Lord you pray.
God might grant this to you or not,
He wants you to trust Him with your lot.

What your greatest need is, He knows best,
and maybe it is that you should have a rest.
But when one day new energy surprises you,
full of joy you are amazed at how much work you can do.

You wish all your days could be like this
assuming wrongly, that life might be unending bliss.
So, let us accept thankfully all of God's ways,
both when we are energetic or tired and slow are our days.

58. My Dreams for the New Year 2006

A New Year is approaching in a few days;
although I am 83 years of age, can I still change my ways;
can I still dream and have a goal;
can I still hope to become whole?

The answer is an affirming 'Yes',
at any stage of life, God wants us with growth to bless.
He wishes that fully life we embrace,
which only is possible through His wonderful grace.

For the New Year my goal is
not to murmur about duties I find difficult to do,
but rather to be grateful that I don't have to wear
other people's more hurtful shoe.
I aspire to be more generous in giving
and more compassionate for those
who have difficulty in living.

I like to be more patient when storms
and clouds come my way,
and learn to be utterly honest when I pray.
I, too, desire to love a little more each day my neighbour
and come more and more close to my Saviour.

59. Daily Chores

Do we enjoy our daily tasks,
don't we not consider them more a bore when asked?
We seem to get tired of them more often than not
and like to complain about our lot.

The chores we have to do seem to never have an end,
we'd prefer the hours differently to spend.
Every day we have to prepare the food,
whether we enjoy it or are not in the mood.

We, too, have to take care of our health
and wished our labour would bring more wealth.
Day in and day out seems to be the same
and so often for this we our Creator blame.

We don't see that so richly He provides all our needs,
that wise and loving are all His deeds;
He wants us to cheerfully do our daily task
and Him for strength and endurance ask.

In small things we learn to obey,
so that from God's will we do not stray.
Each step we take brings us closer to our goal
of being more loving, so we become whole.

60. Stolen Moments

Stealing, overall is not to be recommended;
theft of any kind in serious consequences will be ended.
But stolen moments could be for us a lifesaver
from our often exhausting labour.

So let us steal a moment to be grateful for health
or to admire nature's abundant wealth.
Let us steal a moment to thank God for His love
and all the blessings He sheds on us from above.

Let us steal a moment for quietness and joy
in the belief that the Lord desires us to employ.
Let us steal moments for relaxation and rest,
so that we can do our best.

Stolen moments can be indeed a precious thing,
that like beautiful music in our ears might ring.
And, as we can see, stolen moments benefits could bring,
especially, when we are in the will of our heavenly King.

61. Good Friday 2006

In silence Jesus endured insults and mocking,
not giving a sound when men did His flogging.
Of His own free will, the cross He took up
and drank to the last drop His bitter cup.

A criminal the crowd had chosen over the Son of God,
hatred had been the result of this evil plot.
As a weakling they considered mankind's Redeemer
and thought Him only a rebellious dreamer.

Men didn't see that for their sins He gave His life;
they were so utterly blind and continued in their strife.
They rejoiced to see Jesus in pain
and forgot that He healed the sick and the lame.

Yet Jesus' sacrifice ended in glorious victory;
for all times He defeated Satan to set us free.
For all that believe, He opened salvation's door,
and death doesn't need to be feared by them anymore.

62. New Years Eve 2006/2007

The old year comes today to an end
and we are not sure if it wisely was spent.
For some, the year might have been difficult and hard,
for others joy and diligence had brought reward.

But everyone had his problems and trials,
for some it was challenging, for others tiring to walk the
miles.
Our attitude tells us if the year was good or bad,
if our heart was thankful or if too many tears we had.

Hopefully, we all learned our lessons in the year past,
so that we became a little wiser at last.
What the new year will bring, we cannot tell,
we can only hope most of it will be well.

We hope that we are able to please our Heavenly Father
and that more truth and understanding we do gather,
that we get to know better our Creator
and do love more our needy neighbour.

63. The Wonder of our Saviour's birth

As a little baby God's Son entered the world of man,
so that identifying with Him we can.
Angel's choirs sang praises to God at this event,
and shepherds in wonder and awe their time did spent.

They saw the divine baby lying in a stable,
as finding room in an inn His parents were unable.
Jesus surely had a humble beginning
in order many hearts to be winning.

To the poor and rich He became the guiding light,
which shines so brightly in the night.
He grew up like me and you,
obedient to His parents and always true.

To save us from our sins he gave His life,
so that we find peace and don't live with strife.
Our praises to God should never know end
for His abundant love on us He does spend.

64. Life when older

When being old we need more rest,
still we'll be wondering if we did our best.
Even when retired and coming to life's end,
it is not good in laziness our time to spend.

How can we relax when we've not done our daily chores,
even when closed are many doors?
There are still worthwhile activities for those with grey
hair;
we still might be able for a needy neighbour to care.

Despite that in most things we are slow,
we still can learn and be able to grow.
We do not work anymore for pay
and can decide how to spend our day.

When we let the Lord direct us as in a younger year,
then being useless we don't have to fear.
We will see the beauty of little blessings with a different
eye
and look thankfully for our sunset years up to the sky.

65. Waiting

Are there people, who don't mind to wait,
even when their friends might be late?
I think those people are of a special kind,
who stay a whole hour in line and do not mind.

Most of us like to hurry along on our way
becoming frustrated when in a
long line-up they have to stay.
But often waiting does us good,
even when not pleasant is our mood.

By it, the virtue of patience we might acquire
and for this people will us admire.
We might learn not to rush every day
and spend some time to relax and to play.

66. Shedding Tears

When sadness and sorrow come our way
we are shedding tears and might start to pray.
But not only in dark times shall tears cover our face,
there are many tears shed because of God's grace.

Overwhelm us could gratitude and thankfulness,
since God with His abundant love does us so richly bless.
Moist might become our eye
when remembering that Christ did on the cross for us die.

When beauty touches our heart,
with crying we might start.
Tears are not only for healing,
They, too, express our deepest feeling.

67. Morning at Christmas Eve 2007

Christmas Eve is awaiting us tonight
with the Christmas tree and its many a light.
The presents are wrapped and placed under the tree;
they are for all of us, for you and for me.

My husband and I will celebrate with our daughter and
son,
with their spouses and two grandsons, we will have fun.
Even two dogs for the celebration will be there,
who probably only for sausages will care.

But all the activities should never let us forget,
that our Heavenly Father with His greatest gift us met.
He sent Jesus Christ as a baby to earth today
to show us how to live a godly way.

Jesus came to set us free;
for our sins He died on a tree.
He is our Redeemer and only salvation
and should be worshipped by every nation.

Jesus birth shows us God's unlimited love
He showers on us from above.
So, on this Holy Night let us in awe and wonder
before Him stand
and asked Him our sinful hearts to mend.

68. God's Greatest Gift

Christmas 2007

How great a love God showed the human race
as He gave us His Son by His amazing grace.
For this holy child was chosen a stable,
so that those relating to God are enabled.

Over the place of his birth shone a shining star,
which could be seen both near and far.
Wise man came from far away
to worship the Holy Child as in the manger He lay.

That our Saviour was born, their faith let them know,
throughout His life the heart of the Father He'd show.
For He was born to save every one's soul
as He died for our sins to make us whole.

So let us adore this King of kings,
Who Good News to us brings,
and let us give to Him our all
and listen joyfully to His call.

69. New Years Evening 2007/2008

The year 2007 now comes to an end
and I pray that this I did usefully spend.
There have been for me trials about my health,
but God's presence and touch were my wealth.

I hope through my tough lesson I did grow
and in thankfulness to my Saviour my head I bow low.
May I come closer to Him in the next year
and love those more who to me are near.

May I follow my Creator's guidance each day
ever watchful not to wander from the narrow way.
May the joy of the Lord always be my strength,
so I never complain of my journey's length.

May I clearer the beauty of God's creation see,
for which He never has asked any fee.
May I be willing to do His will,
learning contentment and how to be still.

70. "Molly"

Molly is the little dog of Jethro, my 7-year old grandson;
surely, together, they always have lots of fun.
Molly is still a puppy with curly hair,
and she has brown eyes and manners fair.

She loves all people and likes to sit in their laps
to be cuddled whenever she takes her naps.
The food she gets from Jethro's mom,
and for her the work is never done.

But Jethro spends time with Molly playing,
and that they love each other everyone is saying.
He has the most wonderful companion
in this little dog so dear,
and likes when Molly to him is near.

71. A Winter Day

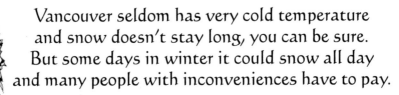

Vancouver seldom has very cold temperature
and snow doesn't stay long, you can be sure.
But some days in winter it could snow all day
and many people with inconveniences have to pay.

Children think the white stuff is fun;
they are happy when they play in it and run.
But older folks think differently,
they would rather in their homes to be.

Into a wonderland the landscape is transformed by snow,
and the branches of the trees are bent low.
Lets not complain when white snowflakes fall from above,
and enjoy the different seasons with love.

72. The Joy of Writing

By writing, your thoughts you can express,
regardless if you enjoy life or it might be a mess.
Paper is patient and doesn't mind what you put down,
though you be in a happy mood or wear a frown.

It's as if talking to a friend,
who listened to you and does you understand.
You might see a problem in a different way,
and it might no longer with you stay.

Joyful moments we don't like to forget,
they are helpful when at times we fret.
When older, we delight to read of our younger days,
and find our journey through life shaped our ways.

73. Murder

Is murder only taking someone's life
because we live with him in strife?
Much more, murder we can call
for instance, when we try our brother to fall.

When through biting words we try to take his hope
so that he might have trouble with his life to cope;
often murderous words are used
by which another is abused.

Indeed, such words kill bit by bit,
though never a bullet used to hit.
Only forgiveness again and again
will help to cope us and stay sane.

74. The Time is Now

God's door to Salvation is open every day,
so that at His feet our whole life we may lay.
Yet there'll be a time when He may shut the door,
so, let us not waste even a single hour more.

The Lord reaches out to us patiently;
His salvation is completely free.
Nevertheless, we are foolish when for
the judgement day we don't prepare
and are not watchful and for our souls don't care.

The foolish virgins ran out of oil;
they had been complacent and didn't toil,
and when the Lord came to seek His own,
they were too late to enter the door to the heavenly throne.

Let us all be warned not to be too late
so that we don't stand for a closed divine gate.
Let us always have oil in our lamp
so that at the end of our life with confidence
before God we stand.

75. Should Cancer scare us?

Cancer for most people is a dreadful word;
being afflicted with it might turn a man to the Lord.
We don't like to waste away;
we like to see another day.

But when we trust in the Almighty God,
we might see different our lot,
that a lesson we have to learn we might see
which brings us closer to Jesus who
was crucified for us on a tree.

The only cancer we should fear
is the sin that for us is so dear.
Sin is a cancer that destroys the soul,
but when we repent, God will make us whole.

So, be not distraught when being ill,
to bless you is God's loving will.
Fear only the cancer of sin that lodges in your heart,
and let the Lord remove it
so that your life has a new start.

76. Don't stop Living when Old

Why do we seem to see mainly
the health problems advanced years do bring
and not the song a life lived well does sing?
We may not hike up mountains anymore,
but still face challenges galore.

Life doesn't end for those with grey hair;
we still can love and for others care.
There are many delights
that in our youth we ignored,
we don't have to stop living and being bored.

Other activities we will have to take up,
and there is no reasons not to see full our cup.
We might not have the strength for many a chore
and might not be able to travel anymore.

Yet, we have the time for a cherished task;
we still can learn and questions ask.
The wonder of living we still can embrace
and delight in God's love and His grace.

77. Repentance

The Lord asks us to repent,
then His outstretched hand He will us lend.
From our sinful ways He wants us to turn 180 degrees
and this doesn't cost us any fees.

It won't be a sudden turn-around,
since we still to sin are bound.
But it will be a growing towards becoming mature
through the difficulties and trials we shall have to endure.

We shall learn each day to love a little more
and come closer to Jesus whom we shall learn to adore.
Though we have to repent again and again,
and sometimes we might think it is all in vain.

But on us the Lord in His patience doesn't give up;
He helps us in our struggles and fills our cup.
He guides us to do His will,
so that joy fills our heart and we become still.

78. What is happening to Christmas?

Happy holidays people now say
and not many anymore pray.
The name of Jesus is avoided more and more
and fewer are the people who the King of kings adore.

People go shopping and eat and drink
and forget that God in Jesus came to earth
redemption us to bring.
Are we now ashamed of our father's faith
and don't see anymore our Creator's gift and grace?

By replacing Christmas for a holiday season,
for hope of salvation then there is no reason.
Though avoiding Jesus Christ's precious name,
He always will be our Saviour and stay the same.

He came to earth to reveal to us the Father above
and to redeem mankind because He does us love.
He came to show us His way
so that we can follow Him and do not stray.

He came to heal and to teach
that through His sacrifice heaven we can reach.
He will always be our light and our Saviour,
and especially at Christmas
let us proclaim this to our neighbour.

79. Let's see our Problems as Challenges

Problems seem to wear us down;
they make us bend and let us wear a frown.
We might think they never would go away
and we stop trying and cease to pray.

Let us as a challenge a problem see,
which does gives us hope to set us free,
that encourages us to work on a task
for which the help of our Heavenly Father we can ask.

A challenge gives our life a meaning;
we have work to do and should stop all this dreaming.
When we go forward on our uphill road,
lighter with each step becomes our load.

As higher we go, clearer becomes our sight
and slowly we will see some light.
Finally, we meet our challenge at last,
and worries and doubts are left in the past.

80. Looking Up

When the road seems steep and hard to climb,
then go slowly and take a rest sometime.
But never forget to go forward still
in the confidence of God's perfect will.

When the night is dark, look up to the sky;
for the reason of darkness we don't always know why.
But let the stars of heaven give you light,
so that you do not stumble in the night.

Look forward to the dawn of the day
and rejoice when the sun again shines on your way.
You wonder why no longer steep seems the road,
until you find from your back the Lord took your load.

Your steps are now firmer and stronger
and you are not tired any longer.
Beautiful sights Jesus does you show,
so that in gratitude your head you bend low.

81. Hatred

Hatred poisons the air,
it occupies a heart that for others
doesn't seem to care,
a heart that is surrounded by a wall of stone
and is empty and alone.

No beauty see those who hate,
and more than often they hurt their mate.
They blame others for being discontent and
rejecting their Maker, who their heart could mend.

Frustration is with them every day
and in their darkness they don't find their way.
Yet there is hope for every soul
if they allow their Redeemer to make them whole.

82. Refocus your Thoughts

When going through problems or trials,
when the road is steep and long seem the miles,
then don't focus that the walk might be difficult and hard,
but instead that dawn comes after a night very dark.

Don't focus that your walk might be slow
but that each day a little more you do grow.
Focus that God is touching you with His guiding hand,
that He doesn't want you to fall, but upright to stand.

Go with confidence your uphill road
and remember that Jesus carries all your load.
Don't focus constantly on your pain,
but on the healing you with the Lord's help will gain.

Always let your thinking be heavenwards
and remember that God wants to soften our stony hearts.
Be thankful that holy He wants you to make,
which is not done in a hurry but a whole life will take.

83. Who is a Hero?

Hero's are difficult to find;
they are people of a special kind.
We admire their courage and their strength,
as their endurance seemed to be of great length.

Do hero's never cry?
I think that would be a lie.
They have weaknesses as we have too,
but they stand firmer in each of their shoes.

They are not only the soldiers who a war do fight,
there are others who shine for us as a light.
A loving mother is a bright example,
who patiently works hours that are ample.

Heroes also we find among the ill
or among those who are persecuted for doing God's will.
A hero seldom is famous or known well,
but their life story let's of their courage tell.

The strength which a hero does need
comes from obeying the Lord's loving lead.
Trust in our Redeemer courage it does give,
so in His presence always let us live.

84. Reaching the End of a Tunnel

To be in a tunnel can be scary and dark;
there we won't hear the song of a lark.
Even our footsteps we cannot see
and we wish, that there we wouldn't be.

In the darkness we might try
to call out to the Lord with our cry,
that to the tunnel's end He will us guide,
so that again we see the light.

Surely, He will reach out to us His hand,
because, we can be assured, He is our friend.
Daylight, at last, we see again
and know that our prayer had not be in vain.

A new song is in our heart
and hope and life seem to have a new start.
So, you can be sure at the end of each tunnel is light
where God will lead us by His love and might.

85. Depending on the Lord

Depending on God's guidance and leading,
by studying His Word and each day reading
helps us to live pleasing Him with our life;
to have joy and contentment and not much strife.

That doesn't mean to be slothful and lazy,
to assume so, are thoughts that are crazy.
Diligent we should be from the start
and never give up from working hard.

By never straying from our Creator's will,
we will be successful and peace our heart will fill.
And if our goal is to do our best,
then we should not forget between work to rest.

And so with our Creator we work hand in hand,
who so richly gives us plentiful talent;
by using it for His glory and pleasure
we'll have a purpose in life we won't regret never.

86. Forgiveness

We often get hurt in life
since true love is rare and there is much strife.
People might not mean to hurt each other,
but harsh words are not seldom used to a brother.

Too many people think their unhappiness
is the fault of those who are to them near
and letting their frustration out on these who are dear.
They don't see into their stony hearts
and that their hurtful words are as fiery darts.

Only by responding with forgiveness will our wounds
heal;
forgiveness is costly, but is the only way
that love for the other person we will feel.
For this, strength we have to ask the Heavenly Father
above,
who so abundantly sheds on us His love.

87. My Friend

Who is my friend?
One who the most expensive presents on me does spend,
one who flatters me about my looks
or the one who has read all kinds of books?

Will I find a true friend in those above,
are they really able to love?
A true friend is not perfect in all his ways,
like me, he has his difficult and joyful days.

A true friend sticks to me like a brother,
he doesn't give up on me when sometime I do him bother.
He accepts me with my virtues and many a fault
and realises that God is still in the process me to mould.

He encourages when I am in the midst of a trial
and goes with me many a mile.
He is open and honest to me
and for this he doesn't charge any fee.

Yet, I shouldn't take for granted when such a friend I meet;
true friendship is rare and always a two way street.
A friend's love for me I should without hesitation return
and then great things we will from one another learn.

88. Open your Eyes

Open your eyes to God's creation;
wonders galore will fill you with elation.
In awe before the beauty of a flower you might have leant,
as for your enjoyment they are meant.

There is so much to admire and to see,
have you noticed the different shades of green on a tree?
Have you seen with an open eye
how beautiful appears the sky?

Are you thankful for the birds so small
or for other animals strong and tall?
Do you stand before majestic mountains in wonder
and let the Lord's creativity you ponder?

Seeing with open eyes is a gift from above,
which God gives us because He is love.
With a lighter step let's walk our way,
when so much beauty we see each single day.

89. Rules

Rules and regulations
are important for all nations.
Otherwise we would have chaos all round
and order would not be anywhere found.

Those who complain about important rules
must realise that they are fools.
How can we live peacefully with each other,
when lack of order does us bother.

Even in our daily living we need to have rules;
they start for a small child when he enters school.
Much valuable time they do us spare
when following them we care.

But rules and regulations can be overdone
and then life becomes rigid and is no fun.
We have to find a middle way
in order to enjoy each day.

90. Acceptance

Life has its sunshine and its rains,
its losses and its gains.
We might be ill or enjoy good health,
we might struggle when poor or have wealth.

It is not always easy to accept what comes our way
and from deliverance of adversity we like to pray;
this may be granted or not
and it is our decision if we accept our lot.

Acceptance of that which we cannot change,
of what might frighten, or seem to be strange
will bring us contentment and peace of mind
which we otherwise might never find.

91. Never stop Dreaming

Dreaming is not a wasteful thing,
it might shape your future and happiness bring.
But just dreaming, not acting toward your dream
could frustration and disappointment mean.

So don't sit back, but slowly your dream start to fulfil,
not forgetting to stay in the Lord's perfect will.
It might be a slow beginning,
but if you stick to it, you will be winning.

Never forget that for your life God has a special plan,
and achieving the impossible with His help you can.
To make your dream come true, never give up,
and in the end, overflowing will be your cup.

92. The Gift of a refreshing Sleep

How wonderful to wake up in the morning
after a refreshing sleep;
it surely, can be considered a special form of treat.
With new energy we start the day
and for this we did not have to pay.

If enjoyed is every task,
for more we really should not ask.
The world seems brighter than on the day past
and we hope this feeling will with us last.

For this we should not forget to thank the Lord,
Who blesses us by action and by word,
Who takes care of us even when not sleeping well;
He is always with us, as the Bible does us tell.

93. A Metaphor for the World

The world on a slippery road is heading down
and people don't realise they could certainly drown.
To the warning signs they are blind;
their hearts are made of stone and confused is each one's mind.

They think they are their own god
and are cold to other peoples lot.
May their eyes be opened before they are engulfed by the
night,
so that they see the stars, which could give them light.

Then they could see that they are steadily going downhill
and they might pause and be still.
They might see that their direction was wrong
and they might learn to pray to God to make them strong.

Now, the uphill way they might find
and learn to others to be kind.
For the first time, joy would fill their heart
and a new life have a start.

94. A Mandatory Day

In our life we all have mandatory days,
when young, middle aged or old, they will change our
ways.
Duties might be done with a cheerful attitude
or we do them in a complaining mood.

Wise parents require their children certain tasks to
perform,
but often this is not the norm.
Then children never responsibilities learn
and have trouble later their living to earn.

Parents of young children have duties galore
and oft they are stressed out and think
they can't handle anymore.
But when they never give up,
in later life blessings might just fill their cup.

When old and our hair is white,
we know what we did wrong or right.
Old age doesn't allow us a strenuous day,
but we are never to old to give thanks
to the Lord and to pray.

95. Stand firm

When rain and storms do you surround,
when in despair and hopelessness you are found,
when you are in the fire of affliction,
stand firm and never give up your conviction.

God wants to make you strong
which can only be achieved through pain,
He doesn't want you to be as vases of glass or porcelain.
Hothouse plants He doesn't want you to be,
but strong as a storm-beaten tree.

Our Creator separates gold from dross and alloy,
because in our life He wants us to have joy.
So let us in every situation stand up tall,
only God knows what is best for us all.

96. Listen

To listen is an art not many people possess,
not realising that by listening the other person we bless.
To really listen is an act of love
for this, we need God's help from above.

When someone needs a listening ear,
but too much time it takes, we fear,
when bombarded with other thoughts is our mind,
full-time attention we're unable to find.

Listening needs ourselves to forget
and to concentrate on the words our friend has said,
so that we can give helpful support,
which certainly would please our Lord.

97. Routines

Routines at times drag us down;
we complain about them and wear a frown.
The chores seem to be the same week after week
and life then for us looks somewhat bleak.

We like a break from the routines so steady,
but for taking risks we are not ready.
Travelling might be too costly or at home we like to stay,
and so we follow our routines day after day.

Yet, this is not so bad after all,
it prevents us from many a fall.
Not adventurous or exciting it may look,
But it doesn't hinder us once in awhile to read a good
book.

Following routines with patience and discipline
could peace of mind for many people mean.
It doesn't prevent from pursuing our gifts from above;
important is that everything is done with love.

98. Stealing

Many people claim to be honest all the way,
but when it comes to income tax
they try not the right amount to pay.
They don't feel any pangs in their heart,
but think by not paying all, they are smart.

Nevertheless, it is as serious
as stealing another's man's money,
and surely it is wrong and not at all funny.
Also, in business, many people are tempted to steal,
and they think they have made a good deal.

How about when finding another's man's treasure
and using it all for your own pleasure?
You can be sure dishonesty never does pay,
and with a guilty conscience to sleep
such a person should lay.

What shall we think of a poor mother
who for her child has no bread,
who is distraught that her children aren't fed,
then, when taking from others would this be right,
would this in the eyes of God be justified?

I don't know the answer for a case like this,
only that in life we can't always expect bliss.
But we can always pray to our Heavenly Father for our
need,
then to the right action He will us lead.

99. A Song in Darkness

Many birds sing their most beautiful songs shortly after
night;
they hope to be better heard than in bright daylight.
Does the noise during the day drown their song
and for more attention our little birds do long?

There are the nightingales and robins
that sing when it's quiet,
which is more difficult when the sun is shining bright.
Do humans have a song in a night very dark,
is then not most of the time cold and fearful their heart?

Even so, there are people who have a song in their
darkness,
who believe that even in affliction the Lord does them
bless.
Their hope kills all the evil darts that do them assault
and in the darkest of night they find peace
in God without doubt.

100. The Mystery of God

Who can understand God's holiness,
who comprehend His justice and His desire to bless,
who can realise the depth of our sin,
and the mercy of God which helps us a new life to begin?

God's wrath can frighten us and hope we might lose,
but we're saved by His grace when repentance we choose.
Our Creator showed us His love by sacrificing His Son,
so that we could be saved and justice be done.

Who can ever understand our Saviour's love,
He so abundantly sheds on us from above?
Through His sacrifice He pursues our souls,
to set us free and make us whole.

CPSIA information can be obtained at www.ICGtesting.com
Printed in the USA
BVOW01s0158010514

352198BV00001B/7/P